WHEN HUMANS UNITE

Abhijit Naskar is the twenty-first century mind of science, whose glorious philosophical touch has enabled modern Neuroscience to effectively engage in the human society towards diminishing the ever-growing conflicts among religions. As an untiring advocate of global harmony and peace, he became a beloved best-selling author all over the world with his very first book "The Art of Neuroscience in Everything". With various of his pioneering ventures into the Neuropsychology of religious sentiments, he has hugely contributed to humanity's attempt of eradicating religious differences, for which he is popularly hailed as a humanitarian who incessantly works towards taking the human civilization in the path of sweet general harmony.

I0415531

WHEN HUMANS UNITE

MAKING A WORLD WITHOUT BORDERS

ABHIJIT NASKAR

When Humans Unite: Making A World Without Borders

Copyright © 2019 Abhijit Naskar

This is a work of non-fiction

An Amazon Publishing Company, 1st Edition, 2019

Printed in the United States of America

ISBN: 9781099237584

Also by Abhijit Naskar

The Art of Neuroscience in Everything
Your Own Neuron: A Tour of Your Psychic Brain
The God Parasite: Revelation of Neuroscience
The Spirituality Engine
Love Sutra: The Neuroscientific Manual of Love
Homo: A Brief History of Consciousness
Neurosutra: The Abhijit Naskar Collection
Autobiography of God: Biopsy of A Cognitive Reality
Biopsy of Religions: Neuroanalysis towards Universal
Tolerance
Prescription: Treating India's Soul
What is Mind?
In Search of Divinity: Journey to The Kingdom of Conscience
Love, God & Neurons: Memoir of a scientist who found
himself by getting lost
The Islamophobic Civilization: Voyage of Acceptance
Neurons of Jesus: Mind of A Teacher, Spouse & Thinker
Neurons, Oxygen & Nanak
The Education Decree
Principia Humanitas
The Krishna Cancer
Rowdy Buddha: The First Sapiens
We Are All Black: A Treatise on Racism
The Bengal Tigress: A Treatise on Gender Equality
Either Civilized or Phobic: A Treatise on Homosexuality
Wise Mating: A Treatise on Monogamy
Illusion of Religion: A Treatise on Religious
Fundamentalism
The Film Testament
Human Making is Our Mission: A Treatise on Parenting
I Am The Thread: My Mission
7 Billion Gods: Humans Above All
Lord is My Sheep: Gospel of Human
Morality Absolute
A Push in Perception
Let The Poor Be Your God
Conscience over Nonsense
Saint of The Sapiens
Time to Save Medicine
Fabric of Humanity

Build Bridges not Walls: In the name of Americana
The Constitution of The United Peoples of Earth
Lives to Serve Before I Sleep

DEDICATION

To the youth of this world

CONTENTS

LOVE ABOVE ALL

ABHIJIT NASKAR

When the mind is without borders, the world will be without borders. And this is only possible if love supersedes all our petty and primitive selfishness. If we don't sacrifice our selfishness at the altar of harmony, we'll have to sacrifice tranquility of our children at the altar of segregation. Once a person makes the sacrifice, the mind opens up to a whole new world of possibilities - a world where anything is possible, all because one human's joy and sorrow will be all humans' joy and sorrow.

It's time that we put an end to all discriminations and segregation once and for all. If we don't foster the courage to speak up and act against discrimination now, then the fall of the entire human civilization is ensured. So, throw away all callousness and indifference, and be empowered with the force of conscience, courage and compassion. Be an embodiment of love and trample every bit of prejudices that you encounter along the way, both within and without.

Only if the humans could realize the inexplicable happiness that comes from loving others, there would no longer be any trace of hatred and discrimination in the world. The highest truth in the world is love. Love trumps all segregation.

But we must keep in mind that here, we are not talking about romantic love. Here, we are concerned with something purer and deeper than mere romantic activity of the sexual psyche. We are concerned with a love, that demands no love in return - we are talking about a love, that demands no praise in return - we are talking about a love, that demands no benefit in return. Such love without benefits is the purest form of love.

I love all women and men everywhere, without letting a single thought of sexual expectation creep into that love. Here, I am not at all insinuating that there can be no involvement of sexual intimacy in love, that is, between partners, rather what I'm pointing out is that, the purpose of love should be the act of love itself, not sexual gratification. Sexual gratification can be a part of love between partners, but it must never be the prime goal.

In its purest form, there is no difference between your love for your companion and that for humanity. Today's so-called love in relationships, goes something like this. Person falls in love, lives together with another person for a while, gets used to the person and falls out of love for that person, to fall in love with another person again. And this goes on till there's any life left in the veins. Humanity has lost the real sense of love in the relentless chase after instant gratifications, and as a result, people today treat people as if there are some replaceable smartphones.

Today's so-called modern human love hails another person as some kind of object, that can be replaced after a while. I disapprove of this kind of replaceable love, for in time such behavior will only beget a society of messed up addicts, who keep running from person to person, not in search of love, but in search of sensory stimuli. It's time that we actually take a stand on a global scale to not advocate for such replaceable love, for, if we don't know the value and irreplaceability of a person, then I'm afraid, we ain't human yet.

It pains me to say this, but there's no love in love any more, that's why even making love loses its magic in no time at all. Making love is not magical if there is no love. Here the thing is, loving someone doesn't mean loving that person with a slight expectation for break-up after a while. Loving a person means loving with all the powers in your spirit, with no consideration for separation whatsoever. Loving someone means giving them the power to kill you, while believing that they won't.

Remember, never give up on love. It is easier to give up in search of a better prize, because the brain always keeps craving for new stimulants, but this way you only keep on searching, never to find peace in love. Let me tell you a story. There was a student who asked his teacher, what is love. The teacher said go into the field and bring me the most beautiful flower. The student returned with no flower at hand and said, 'I found the most beautiful flower in the field but I didn't pick it up for I might find a better one, but when I returned to the place, it was gone.'

We always look for the best in life. When we finally see it, we take it for granted and after some time start expecting a better one, not knowing that it's the best. Seek for your love, and once you have it, never ever give up on it, no matter the situations. Stop taking the easy way out, at every puny obstruction that you encounter. Be a being of character and stick to your love, no matter the situation. You may ask why? Why should you bother with keeping your relationship, when things are not going well! Let me elaborate on the answer, with research done on married couples. Studies have revealed that people who stay married live around four years longer than people who don't.

A good marriage, where both partners are exclusively committed to each other, keeps them healthier both physiologically and psychologically, by directly influencing the nervous system and immune system. In contrast, a divorce can depress the immune system's healthy functioning. And this depression in the system's ability to fight foreign invaders leaves a divorced individual open to more infectious diseases. Not only do happily married people avoid this drop in immune function, but their immune systems keep getting an extra boost by staying married. Happily married couples have a far lower rate of maladies. They also tend to be more health-conscious than others.

In a study, where researchers tested the immune system responses of fifty couples who stayed overnight in the Love Lab, they found a striking difference between those who were very satisfied with their marriages and those whose emotional response to each other was neutral or who were unhappy. The scientists used blood samples from each subject to test the response of the white blood cells, which are the immune system's major defense weapons. In general, happily married men and women showed a greater proliferation of these white blood cells when exposed to foreign invaders than did the other subjects.

They also tested the effectiveness of other immune system warriors - the natural killer cells, which, true to their name, destroy body cells that have been damaged or altered (such as infected or cancerous ones) and are known to limit the growth of tumor cells. Again, subjects who were satisfied with their marriage had more effective natural killer cells than did the others. If the fitness buffs spent just 10 percent of their weekly workout time, working on their marriage instead of their bodies, they would get three times the health benefits they get from running on the treadmill!

In simple terms, make a little effort to work on your relationship, and you will be healthier than usual. Such an effort is not only a sign of a being of character, but when enough people make enough effort to keep their relationship strong and healthy, it would inadvertently create a healthy society. The health of the society is only a reflection of the health of the individual. And, the healthiest practice in the world is the practice of love (not to confuse with intercourse).

Now to look a little wider, in its true form, the love that a humanitarian feels for humanity, is the same love that the person feels for his or her beloved partner in life. In its purest form, there is no separation between romantic love and humanitarian love, for the force of love has no sexual element involved - in fact, it's neither romantic nor humanitarian, it's plain ordinary love.

Now here things get rather intense, so, let's go very slow. What you call romantic love, is not love at all, for, that kind of relationship begins solely on the psychological foundation of sexual attraction. The force of love manifests in such relationship much later, when all pretenses fade away and the two partners no longer feel the need to be anything but themselves. Thus, romance is not love, it's only romance, a kind of mating ritual carried out in the ultimate pursuit of reproduction. In reality, loving someone means loving the person, even if that person is not with you.

True love, as the force for good, has no sexual element to be concerned with. Love is the language known to all humanity. It's the language that consists of care, concern and conscience. It doesn't matter whether you feel it for your partner, your sibling, your parents, or a complete stranger, it's all one and the same force of love. It's as simple as this, loving means giving, not possessing. Hence, love without (expectation for) benefits is the purest form of love.

Forget not - love sees not facts, love sees not reason - love sees not creed, love sees not superstition - love seeks not reward, love seeks not pleasure - love seeks not praise, love seeks not leisure.

With that flame of love, burning bright and glorious, bear every pain my friend - bear every agony, bear every torment, that the path of service has to offer, only then will destiny rise from the ashes of destitute and salute you with utmost veneration. Remember, when calls humanity, all other identities must take a back seat, and so must all desires to have fun with one's life. Someone said to me the other day 'you should have some fun in life, instead of just working all the time'. I replied to the person 'you may have the luxury to have fun, but I can't even dream of having fun while my own humanity is tormented with countless forms of misery.'

When the world is partying, I'm working - when the world is on dates and getting laid, I'm working - when the world is on holidays, I'm working - when the world is celebrating the festivals, I'm working - for humankind to have a healthy and prosperous life, someone's gotta work - someone must make the sacrifices. If everyone were busy having fun, no one would be there to take humanity ahead and upwards. A few lion-hearts must sacrifice their life forgetting fame, fun and fortune, so that the rest of humanity can live.

EITHER PEACE OR POLITICS

Life is precious, but mother nature is the most ruthless of all dictators, who tries her best to trample the tiniest seedling, with devilish fierceness. That's why, civilization can no longer be taken for granted. Right at this very moment, we the human species stand at the crossroads of human evolution, to quite literally write the very direction of that evolution, a faculty which has been denied to all other species.

So, the question is, with such tremendous capacity in your neurons, will you only choose to keep crawling through life quite like animals in the jungle, or will you utilize that force of life for something greater than mere survival! So what, if you die trying! At least you will die with the awareness that you didn't let your life go to waste! Ask yourself this question, what is the point of life, if no trace of you is left after you are gone! Your name must be engraved in bold and vivacious letters upon the hearts of your people, your humanity, nay our humanity, only then will your character find its rightful place under the sun - only then will you turn formless, tribeless and timeless.

Humanity is too expensive - it can't be compromised for our petty little differences. We must, not should, but must stand above and beyond all differences, so that we become the strength to each other, instead of weakness. And in your attempt to do so, many will come in front of you and proclaim you to be either an idealist or an idiot, but mind not the mockery of the mindless, for those who lack insight, are always afraid of progressive action - and those who are afraid of your actions, will never admit that they are afraid, mostly because they themselves wouldn't be aware of their fear, so their brain would only make them criticize you and be an impediment to your footsteps.

So, keep walking, despite the impediment most heavy - keep walking, despite the agony most torturous - keep walking, despite the mockery most foul - just keep walking, for, your walk counts – for, your walk is not just your walk, but the walk of our whole humanity. In your walk, you will encounter countless comments, advise and criticisms, but never give in to any of them, neither to the praise nor to the hate. There's a cliché - "haters will hate", but remember, haters will hate and appraisers will appraise, but the moment you give in to either of them, your downfall will commence.

Communicate with the haters and the appraisers alike whenever you can, but in case of the former, never retaliate hate with hate, and in case of the latter, never let the praise get to your head. Also, when I say, communicate with the haters, I actually mean communicate, that is, without preconceived biases, because just because they hate certain aspects of your opinions or actions, doesn't mean that they are wrong about everything. Even your worst hater has something to teach you. Even the lowliest bigot has something to teach you.

Many people have called me many things - some a thoughtless collectivist, some a religious preacher, and others a radical materialist. But the reality is - I don't advocate for collectivism, for I am the collective - I don't preach religion, for I am religion - and I am no materialist, for I am the matter and I am the spirit. Spirit can't exist without matter and matter can't grow without spirit. And I am the spirit that flows through all of humankind, to remind them of their humanity, whenever prejudices, biases and discriminations begin to take hold of them.

Here the interesting part is that, contrary to the popular belief, prejudices, biases and discriminations have always been there in us, from the very beginning of humankind's rise in a corner of Africa. In fact, conscience, civility and character, these are rather new-born traits of the human psyche, that came to existence very recently, in comparison with the prolonged existence of the primitive traits throughout our evolutionary history, a history that goes back about 3.5 billion years, to the point in history where life on earth existed in the form of one-cell organism.

Our planet formed as a hot mass of molten rock about 4.6 billion years ago. As the earth cooled, much of the water vapor present in its atmosphere condensed into liquid water, which accumulated on the surface in chemically rich oceans.

One scenario for the origin of life is that it originated in this dilute, hot smelly soup of ammonia, formaldehyde, formic acid, cyanide, methane, hydrogen sulfide, and organic hydrocarbons. Whether at the oceans' edge, in hydrothermal deep-sea vents, or elsewhere, the consensus among researchers is that life arose spontaneously from these early waters less than 4 billion years ago. While the way in which this happened still remains a puzzle, one cannot escape a certain curiosity about the earliest steps that eventually led to the origin of all living things on earth, including ourselves. In this case, all we can do is to keep searching and not give in to mystical non-sense, due to our lack of knowledge beyond a certain point. Remember, this threshold of human understanding never remains stagnant, it always keeps moving a step further, turning a little of the unknown into known, bit by bit.

In an attempt to speculate how life might have originated, so far, we scientists have concocted two possible hypotheses. One hypothesis suggests that life may not have originated on earth at all, instead, it may have reached earth from some other planet. This hypothesis is known as the theory of panspermia. Another hypothesis, known as the theory of spontaneous origin, suggests that life evolved spontaneously from inanimate matter, as associations among molecules became more and more complex.

The theory of panspermia proposes that meteors or cosmic dust may have carried significant amounts of complex organic molecules to earth, kicking off the evolution of life. Hundreds of thousands of meteorites and comets are known to have slammed into the early earth, and recent findings suggest that at least some may have carried organic materials.

Most of us scientists tentatively accept the theory of spontaneous origin, that life evolved from inanimate matter. In this view, as changes in molecules increased their stability and caused them to persist longer, these molecules could initiate more and more complex associations, culminating in the evolution of cells around 3.5

billion years ago. These cells got more and more complex over time and eventually gave rise to the wide array of living creatures on earth, including us humans.

Throughout the evolutionary history of all animals, including the humans, one law that has been dominating the world of the living, is "survival of the fittest". And though this drive for survival is something rather innately primitive, it made way for the rise of our modern civilized capacities of the mind, which in turn, would turn out to be a major force for maneuvering all our innate primitiveness. Let me elaborate further. And to do that we have to look at the life of our ancestors, the Australopithecines.

Australopithecines were believed to be scavengers who ate fibrous roots, tubers, seeds, and vegetation. They received more useable calories out of the starchy tubers and vegetable foods than did tree-dwelling chimpanzees. Natural selection favored the genes responsible for the enzyme amylase for grounded hominids because this savanna diet was much more readily available than the ape's diet in the trees.

Occasionally, some of these early hominins may have hunted small prey and broke open bones left by other animals with small pebbles from riverbeds. But they were definitely not efficient hunters even of small animals. Mostly they were foragers who fed off the leftovers from lions and larger cats. They also used bones for digging their roots and fibers. Tool use was not that different from contemporary chimpanzees. Some have estimated their average life span to be 30 years but children and females were particularly vulnerable to the many larger carnivores. It was still not at all a safe environment. However, being upright meant that some of them could wield clubs for protection and carry food and other objects in their hands.

Eventually they left the forest altogether and moved to the savanna where their upright posture helped to see longer distances for scavenging food and watching for predators. Slowly their legs became longer and they developed arches in their feet allowing them to cover more ground than many of their four-legged cohabitants.

While living in the harsh environment of the wild, a very important tool of survival was being next to each other. This is what we call social organization. And our Australopithecine ancestors had a kind of basic social organization. The freaky surrounding compelled the Australopithecines to live in groups. Once they started to live in groups, they required further social skills in order to manage their social relationship, which in turn proved to be an important trigger for the increase in the brain size. By developing social skills the Australopithecines formed alliances and coalitions within the group in order to supervise their survival inside their society as well as outside of it.

With the limited cranial capacity of about 500 cc, the Australopithecines developed the early capacity of self-control. They also developed a kind of emotional communication, which was confined to physical gestures and primitive vocalization. And such communication system had its own headache. Any negative emotional outbreak could disrupt harmony in the group. Such emotional outbreaks were followed by a lot of noises which attracted attention of the predators. Naturally, this created an adaptive pressure for cortical control of emotion and for the emergence of basic social emotions such as sympathy, guilt, and shame which promote cohesiveness. This triggered an increase in the brain size which was mostly in the neocortex that added an extra layer to the whole brain and made room for more neurons.

The more complex the organization of neurons in the brain gets, the more complex the consciousness becomes, for consciousness is the product of the beautiful conversation amongst neurons. And this conversation takes place in the form of electrochemical signaling in the brain. So when the brain stops functioning fully, your consciousness, or to a broader aspect your mind ceases to exist with its unique individualistic qualities. It's like the soothing flow of water. It is only water as long as its internal realm of two atoms of hydrogen and one atom of oxygen, remains intact. If you break that structure which we call H20, it ceases to be water. Likewise, a soul remains a soul, as long as its neural structures remain intact. If you mess with those structures, then the entire personality of the soul may get radically altered. So, to think even further, if those neural structures inside your head stop working, then the soul ceases to exist forever. So, as long as you have a functional brain, you exist, and the moment that brain dies you die.

And that brain holds quite substantial remnants of our primitive past as well as the seeds for a truly civilized and humane future. But that future won't exist unless we stand up today with the force of conscience and character in our veins, outweighing our innate primitive drives of prejudices, bigotry and discrimination.

Be like water my friend - the water doesn't discriminate between a glass made of gold and a glass made of plastic - it just acquires the shape of whichever glass you pour it in – likewise, be one with all humans regardless of their religion, race or social status, for, in oneness lies bliss, in oneness lies progress. No Quran, no Bible, no Gita, no Cow, is greater than the human self. Humanity must supersede everything, if we are to grow together as a civilized and conscientious species, instead of getting ripped apart by our own sectarian stupidity.

However, here's the painful truth of the human society. We have the neurological potential to be truly a wise species, unlike any other, yet we act like the dumbest species on earth. We are so overwhelmed with our utter sense of self-importance that we haven't even noticed that that self-importance has no trace of self-awareness in it, instead it's filled with the primitive filth of arrogance and bigotry - all of which is because we want the world to be at the feet of the all-important self in us, while not even being aware of an elementary fact of the human psyche, that the "self" doesn't exist.

Self is an illusory by-product of the brain's response to the environment, with the purpose of survival of life. However, within the subjective realm of the human mind, due to higher brain capacities, the self is capable of creating its own illusory purpose, in an attempt to provide meaning in life. So, the meaning of human life depends on the humans only. The meaning that we find in our life, is the meaning that our mind creates for us - it's all internal and organic. Life is an organic creation and so is the meaning of life.

The story of life on earth, is the story of meanings. We shed blood of each other, because we found meaning in war - we slaughtered countless lives because we found meaning in being superior to everybody else - and we still keep on fighting with our own kind, because we find meaning in identifying ourselves with the people of our own country, as opposed to the people beyond the borders. We find meaning, in our own nation, as opposed to other nations. We find meaning in our own culture, as opposed to other cultures. We find meaning in our own race, religion and creed, as opposed other races, religions and creeds.

So, regardless of all the advancements that we have made as a smart species, we still remain as tribal as our primal ancestors. The only difference is that they fought amongst each other with bows and arrows and we fight with our pompous and magnificent technological tools. Till this day, whether a nation is powerful or not, is decided based on the size of its military forces. So, how brutal a nation can be, determines how strong a nation is. Here, nationalists might argue that military is imperative to ensure the safety of a nation. And there lies the biggest tribal and primitive mistakes of all.

If we go deeper into the matter of national defense, we shall discover that, military is only a temporary fix for the age-old problems that actually rise from nationalist sectarianism, i.e. tribalism. So, strengthening military power must never be the aim of a civilized society – instead, the aim must be to eliminate every trace of nationalism, so that nobody needs to kill nobody in the name of a nation.

How can a wise species such as humankind be stupid enough to let precious lives go to waste at the borders! You may say, it's rather glorious to die for your nation. And indeed, it may appear as such, but the truth is something uglier than you can imagine. No matter which side of the border wins in the battlefield, precious lives are always lost in the process. And no amount of victory can bring those lives back – no amount of victory can wipe away the tears of a mother, a father or a spouse. What's the point of such victory that brings only destruction!

There is nothing glorious in the death of a soldier - it's only a disgusting reminder of our petty and primitive self-centeredness, that keeps separating us from our own kind, simply because of some illusory borders created by illusory governments. Harsh as it may sound, most politicians in the government don't care about peace or progress either inside their country or out in the world, all they care about is to feel more and more powerful. However, what the society doesn't notice is that, it's the civil servants who run a country, not the politicians. So, if even a thousand civil servants wake up tomorrow, fortified with the spirit of responsibility, and say "no" to all forms of sectarianism, then no politician will have the power to turn nation against nation. It's enough already - we can't keep sacrificing lives of our siblings, of our children, of our friends at the borders, simply to appease the nationalist insecurities of a handful of brain-less chimps. It's one thing to fight together as humanity against the inhuman acts of terrorism, but another to kill each other in the name of nationalist honor.

It is as simple as this. In a civilized society, welfare and warfare cannot go hand in hand. If they do, then I'm afraid, such society is yet to be civilized. And in order to build a truly civilized society, we need, not democratic government, but meritocratic government, the primary characteristic of which will be the sheer absence of politics, for, as I said earlier, a government is not run by politicians, it's run by civil servants, who are appointed on the empirical basis of merit, unlike the politicians, who get elected mainly on the illusory basis of charm and charisma. Take the civil service out of government and the country will collapse, take politics out of government and the country will flourish.

However, here we cannot naively assume that all civil servants are necessarily good and responsible officials and will remain as such, for, no human is immune to corruption, as the seeds of corruption lie within all of us, and in such situation, even bureaucracy can fall prey to the corrupt character of a few civil servants. So, in the absence of politicians, the civil servants would have to be kept circulated from office to office depending on their expertise every five or so years, so that the corruption of a single civil servant doesn't cause a lasting infection in any part of the nation in any manner. And on top of the entire bureaucratic body there ought to be a group of scientists and philosophers to guide them in the right direction in times of need.

A truly united world is possible only with meritocratic government, not with democratic government, not at least until we can make sure that the political candidates have both the merit and character to run a nation. Hard as it may sound, the public doesn't care about the merit or character of the candidate, all they care about is whether the candidate has entertained them enough or has made them feel patriotic enough with their charming speeches filled with nothing but same old sheer sentimentality and a bit of stone-throwing at the opposition. Yet, the whole world is, run by and proud of, such amateur form of representative selection, and we most proudly call it democracy.

Think about it - when you fall sick, you visit a trained doctor - when you travel in the air, the airplane is flown by a trained pilot - but when it comes to choosing a representative, people most proudly and rather audaciously elect any merit-less politician with the most charm and charisma. And it doesn't matter whether you choose a sentimental fool or an authoritarian buffoon as your representative, the result is always the same, that is, absolute panic and chaos. Sheer sentimentality brings along confusion, for it clouds one's judgement. On the other hand, authoritarianism nourishes prejudices, biases and bigotry.

So, the now the question that rises is, what is the way out from this merit-less democratic clap-trap! How can we make the paradigm-shifting change from democratic to meritocratic government? Here, being an idealist won't solve anything, rather, we must look at the problem in the light of our present societal reality.

It takes thousands of people to turn an illegal political order into a democratic injustice. And as it happens, a huge portion of those people are civil servants. So, if even a handful of civil servants stand strong, responsible and conscientious, then no politician has the power in his pea-brain to do injustice to the people.

I give a call today to the civil servants around the world - yours is to serve, not the government, not the politicians, not even the constitution, but the people. You are the first servants of the society. On your shoulders, lies the responsibility of humanity's present and future. If the armed forces are our last line of defense in any corner of the world, then you are our first line of defense in every corner of the world. Injustice must ask your permission before entering the lives of the people. You, civil servants are the first vanguards of the society. So, be responsible, be courageous and be conscientious - be everything, that the politicians can't be with all their empty charm and charisma. Be the leaders, that the politicians have long forgotten to be.

As I have said in *'The Constitution of The United Peoples of Earth'*,

> "The whole civilized world runs on trust - people trust journalists to provide accurate information, doctors to provide accurate treatment, scientists to provide accurate answers and solutions to unanswered questions and unsolved problems, pilots to provide safe and fast air transportation, and so on. So, the integrity of the civilized world is predicated on the integrity of the individual in their chosen field of work."

Which means that the integrity of the administration that runs a nation depends on the individual integrity of civil servants. Now here, we must keep in mind that, the administration is meant to serve the people, not rule them. The government is the servant, not the master, whether that government is officially run by elected politicians or appointed officials.

In a civilized world, nobody is master to nobody, but everybody ought to be responsible for everybody. If we humans are not responsible for our own humankind, then how can we in clear conscience call ourselves human! What is the meaning of human life, I ask you? Is it to be filled with prejudices and bigotry? Is it to be filled with baseless hate and cultural sectarianism? Is it to be a brain-less nationalist or a robotic rationalist? Or is it to be loving, kind and compassionate! It s as simple as this – a little help with a little smile gives meaning to human life. So, be the help to humanity, be the might to humanity, be the light to humanity and be 911 to humanity.

Everyone is mad for something, I am mad for everyone. The world needs madness, a madness for justice, a madness for harmony, a madness for equality, a madness for humanitarian glory. If everyone had the madness for doing good, there wouldn't be any misery in the world. So, be mad, be furious, be rebellious towards every bit of misery, inequality and injustice in the world. Remember, every injustice anywhere in the world is your business, every misery anywhere in the world is your business, every segregation anywhere in the world is your business. Human condition anywhere in the world is your business. Unless you are old and frail, don't sit still any more. Everyone is sitting still cooped up in their tiny illusory cocoon of comfort and that's why the whole world is messed up.

It pains me even more to say, the youth of underdeveloped and developing countries are running to the developed countries in the pursuit of living an opportune and full life, while ignoring the condition of human life in their own country. This won't do, for, it is the prosperity of the world that we must work for, not just the prosperity of one or a few nations. If we are to instill justice, equality and progress in every corner of the world, then the youth, of all people, must stop being indifferent. There is no greater might than the might of the youth.

However, if the educated youth remain indifferent to the problems of this world, the whole human civilization is bound to tarnish. Ten responsible and rational young citizens are sufficient to clean up the mess of a thousand old superstitious citizens.

A corrupt nation is born, not from corrupt politicians or corrupt civil servants, but from corrupt citizens. If the citizens remain responsible and conscientious - in short, if the citizens actually act like humans, instead of just looking like humans, no government running the nation can get corrupt. If a politician or a civil servant is corrupt, it's their fault, but if the politician or the civil servant remains corrupt forever, then it's the fault of the citizens. It's not just about being responsible citizen, rather it's simply about being a responsible human.

People are suffering, what's that to us! Nation is suffering, what's that to us! Society is suffering, what's that to us! The world is suffering, what's that to us! Such mentality has shoved our entire human civilization into the abyss of misery. People around the world have become used to acting like little children, who depend on the government for every single decision of their life. And with such callousness and foolishness of the citizens, we can never construct a meritocratic government to build a nation of character, for there will always be some politician or civil servant most eager to exploit their power over the people - the people who do not know right from wrong, unless they are told by the "government".

So, it's not enough to have conscious politicians, or conscious civil servants, above all that, we need a conscious body of citizens. In practice, it doesn't matter whether the government is run by politicians or civil servants. If the citizens are uncorrupt, then no government can abuse them, but if the citizens are corrupt to their bones, then even the brightest of governments won't be able to solve their problems. A nation with a thousand awakened citizens and a corrupt leader, is much more alive than a nation with an awakened leader and a thousand corrupt citizens.

In theory, we may place the government on a high pedestal, separate from the citizens, but in practice, the government is not separate from the citizens. So, the success of a government, be it democratic or meritocratic, ultimately depends on the citizens. In fact, if the citizens were actually alive in their mind, instead of being walking corpses, with the very power of democracy they can turn their current government into a truly functional meritocratic government, in a few days. But the problem is, the problems of their nation is none of their business. The politicians throw dirt at each other, the citizens throw dirt at the politicians, so everybody is living in dirt. If you want things to change, then stop throwing dirt and act, whether you are a politician, a civil servant or a civilian.

Good government begins with good citizens, for democracy begins with the citizens. In democracy, a leader can lead only by consent of the citizens. So, whatever problem there is with democracy, it all begins with the citizens. Spineless citizens create spineless democracy - a democracy run by a bunch of self-opiniated windbags and busybodies, whereas citizens of merit and character can create a meritocratic democracy, run by meritocratic government, consisting of individuals of merit and character. Here, the merit of the citizens is not about having an extensive knowledge of how to run the nation, rather it is simply to be not swayed by the charm and charisma of the meritless politicians. Which means, in order to have a proper, functional and civilized democracy, politics must be thrown away from government, which can be done by the parliamentary action of ensuring that no candidate nomination is to be accepted by the electoral commission without proper training in administration and peacemaking. This ought to be the founding principle of a civilized democracy.

Our predecessors around the world in the path of service and reform, made a huge progress by establishing democracy as a civilized alternative to the primitive practice of dictatorship. Now, we stand at yet another crossroads of societal progress, where we must replace our current merit-less and childish democracy with the civilized alternative of meritocratic democracy.

But the harsh reality is, no government, run by politics, is going to change the system that put it into power. And, we cannot surgically remove politics from the existing body of government all together, not overnight anyways, unless the majority of the civil servants step in to make that happen, which is perhaps a little more likely than the majority of civilians stepping in.

Which means, we must look at it from a practical standpoint. And the practical way out of a politics-driven democracy is to start from scratch – that is, we must start regional. Creating more and more new parties is not going to solve anything, what will, is complete elimination of party authority. As long as the people allow the parties to have power, no amount of democratic elections is going to establish true peace and harmony within and among nations.

No organization can stay uncorrupt for long, be it a political party, a religious institution or a charity foundation - sooner or later the instinctual evils of greed and cruelty overwhelm the organization, fueled by its authoritative control over people. So, in no circumstances, the people must give power to a party, that is, if they want a safe and united world for their children. Or let me put it another way, if people genuinely do not want to have any more war, then they must not give power to any party. Unless democracy is cleansed of all political impurities, conflicts and wars will keep on festering in one corner of the world or another. And to do that, people must gather together not in the name of a party, rather for a plain ordinary everyday cause.

The problem with creating a political party is that, by the time you finish creating it, you forget why you created it in the first place. Then slogans replace action and manifestos replace motion. So, forget parties and take action to solve the issues of your society. Come together for a common cause, seek out a leader of merit and character, then act together. And when enough regions of a nation have enough non-partisan, acting leaders of merit and character, the entire democracy of that nation is bound to turn meritocratic. Then only will we witness the rise of true democracy - a democracy free from political authoritarianism - a democracy of the people, by the people, for the people.

Unless we rid this world of politics, there will never be peace. No party can ensure peace, progress and harmony in the world, because to do that, they'd have to step beyond party politics, which would mean placing people before party, that would in turn rock the very foundation of their existence. If any party is capable of placing people before itself, then it wouldn't have been born in the first place. An individual when burning with the desire to change the society, can sacrifice the self in the service of others, but not a party. Because if one person in a party wants to do something for the society, that may essentially jeopardize the party's existence, hundreds of other people in that party will restrain that person from accomplishing what he or she wants to achieve. Then the person may simply jump over to another party, but after some time he or she will face the same sequence of events.

In order to bring a radical lasting change in the society, one must first be free from the shackles of party politics all together. You may create a new party and somehow succeed in doing good to the society throughout your lifetime, but once that party is bigger than you, its loyal followers will no longer place people before the party. It is a neuropsychological impossibility. Over time a person involved in a party, automatically begins to identify the self with the party - the party becomes an irrefutable source of comfort and security for that follower in his or her mind. Naturally, the brain puts various defense mechanisms to practice in the pursuit of protecting that identity at all costs. A huge part of these defense mechanisms is the development, nourishment and functioning of biases. In simple terms, a person involved in one party, neurologically gets conditioned to foster either implicit or explicit hate and prejudices against people who follow other parties. And this is true not just for the followers of political parties, but for followers of any kind of institution. It is a universal neurological phenomenon of the human species.

Take the religious fundamentalists for example. They identify themselves, more with their religion, their scripture, their messiah or prophet, than they do with the human race. They live in a state of constant euphoria, the kind you get when you fall in love. Except here, unlike in the early stage of love, that euphoria never wears off from the psyche of the fundamentalists, rather every argument from the rational world makes their delusion grow more neural interconnections, thus making it even stronger in the fundamentalist brain.

Any kind of refutation of a person's fundamentalist beliefs makes the beliefs only stronger. Repudiation reinforces beliefs, whether they belong to a religious fundamentalist, political fundamentalist or radical rationalist. Everyday challenges that the person faces against his or her religious ideology, only strengthen that ideology even more. That is why, rational thinking of any kind can never break the fundamentalist beliefs of a person, no matter how many logical or scientific arguments are put forward. In short, if you could reason with a fundamentalist, there would be no fundamentalists in the world.

Fundamentalism acts as the mainstream fuel for acts of terrorism carried out in the name of religion. The moment fundamentalism disappears from the face of earth, society would finally get rid of religious terrorism. Terrorism is born of fundamentalism, not of religion. Hence, to get rid of religious terrorism, it is not enough to kill a bunch of Jihadis or Holy Warriors, even though it may be morally justified to do so, for saving humanity from their wrath. Holy War would keep festering one way or another, until religious fundamentalism is eradicated from the human society.

In a civilized society, diversity in religious orientation should be the reason for celebration, not the cause for hatred and differentiation. Religion is a language, if you can speak it, it's a bridge, if not, then it's a barrier. Here, the problem is, people tend to believe that their own language is the only true language, therefore they don't need to learn to speak another one, let alone understand the sentimental significance of that language in people's lives. Thus, religions around the world have only created barriers among people.

But we stand today at such a significant crossroads that we can't simply ignore such sectarian acts as naïve cultural differences. Rather, we must, not should, but must attempt to break down those barriers. Now, here one may wonder, how can we do so, without causing further violence and disorder in the society! And indeed, this is the reason why many of the religious moderates simply choose to ignore a person's religious bigotry. They simply don't want more trouble.

However, the harsh reality is, by choosing to remain silent, one may avoid trouble for oneself, but that won't save our children and their children from facing bigotry-induced prejudices in the future. In this case, silence is not a sign of civility, rather it's a sign of primitiveness. It's primitive, because by staying silent, you are accepting and making way for primitiveness. So, we must break our silence first, in order to break the barriers of religion.

Now, there are two steps that we can take to break these barriers. The first is to recognize and dismantle the primitive traits that have been passed on to us by our ancestors as our religion. Then, we must incorporate a few traits from other religions into our everyday walk of life. The more you want to learn about others without bias, the more they'll want to learn about you. And with this mutual drive for acceptance and understanding, will we construct the world of one humanity.

Right now, we have a world of many humans, but not one humanity. We will be able to call it a world of one humanity, only when the humans genuinely begin to call themselves human above all else. In a recent interview, I was asked, what has been my biggest success. My reply was, "success for me will be the day when all humans everywhere will stand up with a sense of unity and call themselves human, above everything else." This unity lies in assimilation - it lies in non-differentiation - it lies in non-duality.

No amount of religious, nationalist or cultural pride can bring unity in this human world.

Because the price of unity is the sacrifice of one's own pride - pride in every form, be it in the self, in the culture, in the nation or in the religion. Pride is poison, for once you open your doors to pride, more windows of prejudices and bigotry get opened automatically. It is a subconscious process, that programs your mind to protect your own little tribe, called culture or nation, at all costs – even at the cost of slaughtering others.

For every word of pride that you utter about your nation, you send out ten behavioral cues of condescension to others. And that condescension begets more condescension from others, giving rise to a whole lot of prejudices. Thus, we the humankind get ever-lastingly stuck in the whirlpool of pride and prejudices. Pride and prejudice are bffs, wherever one goes, the other follows. And as remnants of our tribal past, they repel all possibilities of assimilation. So, unless you cut them off from your life, harmony will never be a part of our global life.

In short, assimilation begets assimilation, differentiation begets differentiation. So, make your choice. And yes, you do have a choice indeed. The choice is between a human world and an animal world. The former is run by the civilized principle of acceptance, whereas the latter is run by the primeval law of "kill or be killed." If you choose the former over the latter, then you would have to foster the capacity to be aware of your beliefs. Because if you let your beliefs run rampant in your psyche, then it'd only bring separation between you and the rest of humanity. To build a peaceful world, one must rise above one's beliefs.

However, the human mind cannot live without beliefs, which means that we are not aiming for a belief-less society. Beliefs themselves are not necessarily the problem here. The problem is giving the authority of one's life to one's beliefs. Once beliefs are in control of your life, even when you commit the worst kind of atrocities, you won't be aware it, for your brain would make you blind to all the negative aspects of your beliefs. So, you must never let your beliefs be in control of your life. Possess your beliefs, be aware of your beliefs, and put them to practice as per the need, but be very cautious.

This is only possible, if the actions to serve the society, are the actions of an individual and not of a party. An individual can keep his or her beliefs and biases in check, if willing, but not a party. The very functioning of a party takes place under the authority of biases, born to serve an ideology and not people.

To serve the people, you don't need a party, your mind and body are enough. And in doing so, you may fail quite often, but remember, failing doesn't mean stopping. Failure is the first success. The difference between leaders and the masses is in the level of tolerance for failure - in the masses it's microscopic, whereas in legends, there is none, as they do not see failures as enemies, rather as prized possessions.

In reality, there are no such things as failures, but only circumstances that you must go through, before you start to reap the fruits of your toil. So, start the toil - toil for your people - toil for your neighborhood - toil for your society. We must toil our way out from this misery and prejudice infested world of ours. We can even reach Alpha Centauri if we take a few steps ahead every day together. Mark you, we must all hang together, or else, we'll all be hanged separately.

UNITY BREEDS HARMONY

Unity breeds progress and harmony, whereas divisiveness creates regress and disharmony. And this disharmony and regress won't stop unless the humans learn to feel, think and behave like humans. The way to peace is acceptance. One bridge of acceptance trumps a hundred walls of discrimination.

People keep wishing for something good to happen to this world. And if everybody only keeps wishing, then nothing good will ever happen to this world. So, stop wishing and be the good that needs to happen to this world. Remember, mothers and fathers are born everywhere. What the world needs are leaders. Wake up, rise and lead - lead not as an authority, but as a servant – lead not to start wars, but to put an end to all wars, once and for all. One who stops a war before it starts, is the real victor. Be the victor with a strong character and a gentle soul.

Violence is in our DNA, so is Peace. It's our will that determines which one comes to action. Make your decision, for, upon your decision the fate of our people is predicated - there is no time to waste. I feel a storm brewing - a storm of prejudices, bigotry and baseless hate and sectarianism. Unless you decide to be the peace incarnate of your corner of the world, that storm will turn into a Category 5 Hurricane in no time and it will destroy all happiness and tranquility in our children's lives.

If we live in chaotic times, that's our ancestors' fault, but if our children also have to live in chaotic times, then it'll be our fault. So, don't make the mistake of staying indifferent to the problems of the world. We can't blame our ancestors, firstly because they had limited resources, and secondly because blaming won't solve anything. We on the other hand, live in the most resourceful period in human history. We are the most resourceful, tactful and powerful species on Earth, yet the one thing that we are not, is the most peaceful species.

All our achievements have made us the masters of this planet, but unbeknownst to all, in the pursuit of mechanical greatness, we ourselves have turned into a peaceless, mechanical species in pieces. We have placed all our attention on everything except the one thing that makes us who we are, i.e. the human mind. In the pursuit of sustaining order in the external world, we are lost in disorder internally. Silence, serenity and sanity have become alien concepts for us. However, no matter how alien these notions may appear, they are born from the protoplasmic realm of our brain, not as mere notions or concepts to debate over, but as fundamental traits of the human psyche.

But the point is, in the protoplasmic realm of the mind, alongside silence, there lies noise - alongside serenity, upheaval - alongside sanity, insanity. The human mind is a hodge-podge of all things primitive and all things civilized. So, good and evil are both in the nature of the creature known as human. It's in the nature of the humans and the entire animal kingdom to return blow for blow, cheating for cheating, lie for lie, to hit back with all our might. But what makes us true humans is the power to not hit back.

Here, we must ask a rather quintessential question. Why is there in us the desire to do evil in return for evil done to us! Why does this apparently criminal desire even exist? To understand this, we must investigate the very basis of criminal behavior. Every human behavior that we consider evil or criminal, rises from the basic instinctual mechanism of self-preservation. Hate, bigotry, prejudices, discrimination - all of these are product of the biological drive for self-preservation. All crimes are the product of this drive.

Every organic act or phenomenon that persists in nature, one way or another, serves an evolutionary purpose. So, what is the purpose that crime serves, for, if it didn't, then it would have gone extinct long ago! All actions that are considered to be crime in the human world, rise from the biological drive for self-preservation. In short, crime is an evolutionary process. Our ancestors survived in the wild by committing the very acts which we today term as crime. They gathered food through crime, they procreated forcefully through crime, they basically stayed alive through crime. Because that's how things work in the wild.

Crime is the way of life in the wild. The kingdom of the wild is run by only one principle, and that is, survival of the worst criminal, which you would commonly know as "survival of the fittest". What we call crime in the civilized world, is a criterion for survival in the jungle. In fact, we all exist today because of the crimes committed by our wild ancestors at some point in the past. This way, we are all born of crime.

Crime is driven by the biological force of self-preservation. So, unless the humans learn to step beyond selfishness, crime will keep on festering. However, here we must also keep in mind that a huge portion of the criminal offences in the human society occur from anomalous brain activity. So, promoting brain health ought to be a primary concern of all humans across the globe. It's not an optional matter or a matter of doctor's recommendation, rather it is imperative that we take brain health as seriously as we take human rights and justice.

Brain health is not to be hailed as a habit of the rich and famous, rather it must be made a worldwide trait of human existence. A healthy brain is capable of keeping its primitive self-preservation mechanism from going overboard, but when an anomalous brain activity occurs, the self-preservation mechanism is very likely to go into overdrive.

When that self-preservation mechanism becomes extremely unstable and uncontrolled, we encounter some of the most extraordinary and weirdest crimes, that can be placed in either of two categories - psychotic or psychopathic. Here, the first thing that we must point out is, psychosis or psychotic outbursts can be treated with modern medical intervention, whereas, we haven't yet discovered any medical means to treat psychopathy. Crimes committed in a state of psychosis take place due to temporary malfunction of inhibition in the brain, that can be treated with modern medicinal means, whereas the disinhibition in the psychopathic brain is till now untreatable.

Now, these two categories cover mostly the extreme events of crime. But, the world is also filled with various everyday crimes that occur simply due to the everyday lack of self-control, or due to circumstantial pressure. So, the only way forward is to step beyond selfishness, while nourishing our internal capacity of self-control or self-regulation. In this context, let me bring up an excerpt from my treatise on monogamy, to peek into the significance of self-regulation in human society.

> "A man squanders his money on gambling. A woman beats her child. A drunk driver causes a crash that destroys three cars and injures several pedestrians. A student postpones studying until the night before the test and gets a bad grade. A young couple engages in unprotected sex and creates an unwanted pregnancy. A delinquent shoots an acquaintance during an argument. A girl breaks a promise and betrays a friend's confidence. What these disparate events have in common is failure of self-restraint or self-regulation. When self-regulation works well, it enables people to alter their behavior so as to conform to promises, ideals, values and other standards of

human life. When it fails, a broad range of human problems and misfortunes can arise. Self-regulation is thus a key to wellbeing in human life.

Self-regulation is not simply a moral characteristic. It is biologically healthy for both your mind and the body. Which means, those who practice self-restraint have better physical and psychological health. Countless studies have revealed that people with high scores on self-control were better off than those with low self-control on virtually everything. They had better grades in school. They had better relationships with family and friends - less conflict and more cohesion. They were better able to understand others and scored higher on empathy. They showed better psychological adjustment, including fewer psychological problems, fewer signs of serious psychopathology, and higher self-esteem. Not surprisingly, they reported fewer impulse control problems, such as overeating and problem drinking. They had healthier emotional lives, such as being better at managing their anger, and being more prone to guilt than shame. They had less juvenile delinquency.

Other work using the same scale has confirmed the benefits. Supervisors who score higher in self-control are rated more favorably (e.g., as fairer) by their subordinates. People with high self-control make better relationship partners, especially because they are better able to adapt to partners... Thus, effective self-regulation can be recognized as an important key to "success" in life."

-   *Wise Mating: A Treatise on Monogamy*

However, here one must not confuse self-regulation to be the destination. It's only the early step in the path of selflessness. Selflessness is not self-denial, for, those who have to deny the self to serve others, can never be selfless, and those who are selfless need not deny the self. To be selfish is human nature, but to be selfless is humanity. To think of oneself before others is human nature, but to place others before the self is humanity. To weep in trouble is human nature, but taking trouble to wipe someone's tears is humanity.

Hoist your heart and light up the lives, for darkness is upon us and humanity is in peril.

Wash out the darkness like the scarlet sun - be the cloud and run towards the thirsty land to drench it with your soothing monsoon - be the breeze and share happiness with others beyond all petty selfishness. Grab your selfishness by the throat and leave not till it's incapacitated. Remember, streets can have speed limit, but not kindness - ATMs can have withdrawal limit, but not compassion - tests can have time limit, but not conscience.

Try for once to be limitless in kindness, boundless in compassion, timeless in conscience, and you'll discover, there's no bigger happiness than this. The biggest tragedy is to think that the trouble of others is no loss of ours. Once this mentality perishes, there will no longer be any tragedy that we the humans couldn't overcome, for, everybody's loss will be everybody's business.

People among people, such should be the way of life in a civilized society, not people against people. After all, when people stand with people, only then people can call themselves people, and if people can't stand with people, instead, they choose to stand against people, then what right do people have to call themselves people! People need people to progress. There's no greater love than to lay down one's life for the upliftment of the people. And this means, standing firm on the grounds of rights, equality, freedom and sanity, despite being burnt to ashes.

Either burn me or burn with me. But take a stand, for better or for worse. However, I am not asking for absolute sacrifice from everyone. If you feel like doing it, you'll do it anyways - but most humans are not in a situation to sacrifice everything in order to serve others. The point is, even if you are not practically capable of sacrificing all, do your part, no matter how little. Remember, tiny little drops of water, when come together, can produce a majestically ginormous ocean. So, make your tiny little acts of kindness - acts of conscience - acts of change, each day of your life. A meaningful life is a life lived for others - a religious life, is a life lived for others - a human life, is a life lived for others.

There is no greater truth than this - there is no greater reality than this.

BIBLIOGRAPHY

Aristotle. Politics. Penguin; Revised, Reprint edition. (2000)

Aristotle. Physics. Kessinger Publishing, 2004

Adolphs R (2003) Cognitive neuroscience of human social behaviour. Nature Rev Neurosci 4: 165–178.

Adolphs R, Damasio H, Tranel D, Cooper G, Damasio AR (2000) A role for somatosensory cortices in the visual recognition of emotion as revealed by three-dimensional lesion mapping. J Neurosci 20: 2683–2690.

Adolphs R, Tranel D, Damasio AR (2003) Dissociable neural systems for recognizing emotions. Brain Cogn 52: 61–69.

Afton, A. D. (1985). Forced copulation as a reproductive strategy of male lesser scaup: A field test of some predictions. - Behaviour 92, p. 146-167.

Allison T, Puce A, McCarthy G. (2000) Social perception from visual cues: role of the STS region. Trends Cogn Sci 4: 267–278.

Andresen, Jensine, and Robert Forman, eds. Cognitive Models and Spiritual Maps. Bowling Green, Ohio: Imprint Academic, 2000.

Ashbrook, James, and Carol Albright. The Humanizing Brain: Where Religion and Neuroscience Meet. Cleveland, OH: Pilgrim Press, 1997.

Azari, Nina, Janpeter Nickel, Gilbert Wunderlich, Michael Niedeggen, Harald Hefter, Lutz Tellmann, Hans Herzog, Petra Stoerig, Dieter Birnbacher, and Rudiger Seitz. "Neural Correlates of Religious Experience." European Journal of Neuroscience 13, no. 8 (2001)

Agar, N. (2004). Liberal eugenics: In defence of human enhancement. London: Blackwell Publishing.

Alteheld, N., Roessler, G., Vobig, M., & Walter, R. (2004). The retina implant new approach to a visual prosthesis. Biomedizinische Technik, 49(4), 99–103.

Antal, A., Nitsche, M. A., Kincses, T. Z., Kruse, W., Hoffmann, K. P., & Paulus, W. (2004a). Facilitation of visuo-motor learning by transcranial direct current stimulation of the motor and extrastriate visual areas in humans. European Journal of Neuroscience, 19(10), 2888–2892.

Augustine JR (1996) Circuitry and functional aspects of the insular lobe in primates including humans. Brain Res Rev 22: 229–244.

Barash, D. P. (1977). Sociobiology of rape in mallards (Anas platyrhynchos):

Responses of the mated male. - Science 197, p. 788-789.

Barthalomew, G. A. (1970). A model for the evolution of pinniped polygyny. - Evolution 24, p. 546-559.

Berger, J. (1986). Wild horses of the great basin: Social competition and population size. - The University of Chicago Press, Chicago.

Birkhead, T. R., Johnson, S. D. & Nettleship, D. N. (1985). Extra-pair matings and mate guarding in the common murre Uria aalge. - Anim. Behav. 33, p. 608-619.

Beauregard, Mario, and Vincent Paquette. "Neural Correlates of a Mystical Experience in Carmelite Nuns." Neuroscience Letters 405, no. 3 (2006)

Benson, Herbert. Timeless Healing: The Power and Biology of Belief. New York: Scribner, 1996

Bogen, J.E.(1995a), 'On the neurophysiology of consciousness: Part I. An overview', Consciousness and Cognition, 4.

Bogen, J.E. (1995b), 'On the neurophysiology of consciousness: Part II. Constraining the semantic problem', Consciousness and Cognition, 4.

Bremner, J. D., R. Soufer, et al. (2001). "Gender differences in cognitive and neural correlates of remembrance of emotional words." Psychopharmacol Bull 35 (3).

Brothers, L. (2002). The social brain: A project for integrating primate behavior and neurophysiology in a new domain. In J. T. Cacioppo et al. (Eds.), Foundations in neuroscience. Cambridge, MA: MIT Press.

Buss, D. D. (2003). Evolutionary Psychology: The New Science of Mind, 2nd ed. New York: Allyn & Bacon.

Buss, D. M. (1989). "Conflict between the sexes: Strategic interference and the evocation of anger and upset." J Pers Soc Psychol 56 (5).

Buss, D. M. (1995). "Psychological sex differences. Origins through sexual selection." Am Psychol 50 (3).

Buss, D. M. (2002). "Review: Human Mate Guarding." Neuro Endocrinol Lett 23 (Suppl 4).

Buss, D. M., and D. P. Schmitt (1993). "Sexual strategies theory: An evolutionary perspective on human mating." Psychol Rev 100 (2).

Blakemore SJ, Decety J (2001) From the perception of action to the understanding of intention. Nature Rev Neurosci 2: 561.

Bruce C, Desimone R, Gross CG (1981) Visual properties of neurons in a polysensory area in superior temporal sulcus of the macaque. J Neurophysiol 46: 369–384.

Buccino G, Binkofski F, Fink GR, Fadiga L, Fogassi L, Gallese V, Seitz RJ, Zilles K, Rizzolatti G, Freund HJ (2001) Action observation activates premotor and parietal areas in a somatotopic manner: an fMRI study. Eur J Neurosci 13: 400–404.

Buccino G, Vogt S, Ritzl A, Fink GR, Zilles K, Freund HJ, Rizzolatti G (2004) Neural circuits underlying imitation of hand actions: an event related fMRI study. Neuron 42: 323–34.

Calder AJ, Keane J, Manes F, Antoun N, Young AW (2000) Impaired recognition and experience of disgust following brain injury. Nature Neurosci 3: 1077–1078.

Carey DP, Perrett DI, Oram MW (1997) Recognizing, understanding and reproducing actions. In: Jeannerod M, Grafman J (eds) Handbook of neuropsychology. Vol. 11: Action and cognition. Elsevier, Amsterdam.

Carr L, Iacoboni M, Dubeau MC, Mazziotta JC, Lenzi GL (2003) Neural mechanisms of empathy in humans: a relay from neural systems for imitation to limbic areas. Proc Natl Acad Sci USA 100: 5497–5502.

Changeux JP, Ricoeur P (1998) La nature et la règle. Odile Jacob, Paris.

Cochin S, Barthelemy C, Roux S, Martineau J (1999) Observation and execution of movement: similarities demonstrated by quantified electroencephalograpy. Eur J Neurosci 11: 1839– 1842.

Churchland, P.S. (1986), Neurophilosophy (Cambridge, MA: The MIT Press).

Churchland, P.S. & Ramachandran, V.S. (1993), 'Filling in: Why Dennett is wrong', in Dennett and His Critics: Demystifying Mind, ed. B. Dahlbom (Oxford: Blackwell Scientific Press).

Churchland, P.S., Ramachandran, V.S. & Sejnowski, T.J. (1994), 'A critique of pure vision', in Large- scale Neuronal Theories of the Brain, ed. C. Koch & J.L. Davis (Cambridge, MA: The MIT Press).

Crick, F. (1994), The Astonishing Hypothesis: The Scientific Search for the Soul (New York: Simon and Schuster).

Crick, F. (1996), 'Visual perception: rivalry and consciousness', Nature, 379.

Crick, F. & Koch, C. (1992), 'The problem of consciousness', Scientific American, 267.

Craig AD (2002) How do you feel? Interoception: the sense of the physiological condition of the body. Nature Rev Neurosci 3: 655–666.

Damasio, A (2003a) Looking for Spinoza. Harcourt Inc. Damasio A

(2003b) Feeling of emotion and the self. Ann NY Acad Sci 1001: 253–261.

d'Aquili, Eugene. "Senses of Reality in Science and Religion." Zygon 17, no 4 (1982)

d'Aquili, Eugene. "The Biopsychological Determinants of Religious Ritual Behavior." Zygon 10, no. 1 (1975)

d'Aquili, Eugene. "The Myth-Ritual Complex: A Biogenetic Structural Analysis." Zygon 18, no. 3 (1983)

d'Aquili, Eugene, and Andrew Newberg. The Mystical Mind: Probing the Biology of Religious Experience. Minneapolis: Fortress Press, 1999.

Daly DD. 1958. Ictal affect. Am J Psychiatry.

Damasio, A. (1994) Descartes' Error: Emotion, Reason and the Human Brain. New York, Putnams.

Damasio, A. (1999) The Feeling of What Happens: Body, Emotion and the Making of Consciousness. London, Heinemann.

Darwin, C. (1859) On the Origin of Species by Means of Natural Selection. London, Murray.

Darwin, C. (1871) The Descent of Man and Selection in Relation to Sex. London, John Murray.

Darwin, C. (1872) The Expression of the Emotions in Man and Animals. London, John Murray; also published 1965, Chicago, University of Chicago Press.

Dawkins, M.S. (1987) Minding and mattering. In C. Blakemore and S. Greenfield (eds) Mindwaves. Oxford, Blackwell, 151-60.

Dawkins, R. (1976) The Selfish Gene. Oxford, Oxford University Press; a new edition, with additional material, was published in 1989.

Dawkins, R. (1986) The Blind Watchmaker. London, Longman.

Di Pellegrino G, Fadiga L, Fogassi L, Gallese V, Rizzolatti G (1992) Understanding motor events: A neurophysiological study. Exp Brain Res 91: 176–80.

Deikman, A.J. (2000) A functional approach to mysticism. Journal of Consciousness Studies 7(11-12), 75-91.

Delmonte, M.M. (1987) Personality and meditation. In M. West (ed.) The Psychology of Meditation. Oxford, Clarendon Press, 118-32.

Dennett, D.C. (1976) Are dreams experiences? Philosophical Review 73, 151-71; also reprinted in D.C. Dennett (1978) Brainstorms: Philosophical Essays on Mind and Psychology. Harmondsworth, Penguin, 129-48.

Dennett, D.C. (1987) The Intentional Stance. Cambridge, MA, MIT Press.

Dennett, D.C. (1988) Quining qualia. In A.J. Marcel and E. Bisiach (eds) Consciousness in Contemporary Science. Oxford, Oxford University Press, 42-77.

Dennett, D.C. (1991) Consciousness Explained. Boston, MA, and London, Little, Brown and Co.

Dennett, D.C. (1995a) Darwin's Dangerous Idea. London, Penguin.

Dennett, D.C. (1995b) The unimagined preposterousness of zombies. Journal of Consciousness Studies 2(4), 322-6.

Dennett, D.C. (1995c) Cog: steps towards consciousness in robots. In T. Metzinger (ed.) Conscious Experience. Thorverton, Devon, Imprint Academic, 471-87.

Dennett, D.C. (1995d) The path not taken. Behavioral and Brain Sciences 18, 252-3; commentary on N. Block, On a confusion about a function of consciousness. Behavioral and Brain Sciences 18, 227.

Dennett, D.C. (1996a) Facing backwards on the problem of consciousness. Journal of Consciousness Studies 3(1), 4-6.

Dennett, D.C. (1996b) Kinds of Minds: Towards an Understanding of Consciousness. London, Weidenfeld & Nicolson.

Dennett, D.C. (1997) An exchange with Daniel Dennett. In J. Searle (ed.) The Mystery of Consciousness. New York, New York Review of Books, 115-19.

Dennett, D.C. (1998) The myth of double transduction. In S.R. Hameroff, A.W. Kaszniak and A. C. Scott (eds) Toward a Science of Consciousness: The Second Tucson Discussions and Debates. Cambridge, MA, MIT Press, 97-107.

Dennett, D.C. (1998b) Brainchildren: Essays on Designing Minds. Cambridge, MA, MIT Press.

Dennett, D.C. (2001) The fantasy of first person science. Debate with D. Chalmers, Northwestern University, Evanston, IL, February 2001.

Dennett, D.C. (2003) Freedom Evolves. New York, Penguin.

Dennett, D.C. and Kinsbourne, M. (1992) Time and the observer: the where and when of consciousness in the brain. Behavioral and Brain Sciences 15, 183-247, including commentaries and authors' responses.

Dewhurst, Kenneth, and A. W. Beard. "Sudden Religious Conversions in Temporal Lobe Epilepsy." British Journal of Psychiatry 117 (1970)

Dewhurst K, Beard AW. Sudden religious conversions in temporal lobe epilepsy. 1970 Epilepsy Behav 2003

Devinsky O, Lai G. Spirituality and religion in epilepsy. Epilepsy Behav 2008.

Devinsky, O., Morrell, MJ, Vogt, BA. (1995) 'Contribution of anterior cingulate cortex to behavior', Brain, 118.

Eckhart Meister, Selected Writings

Fadiga L, Fogassi L, Pavesi G, Rizzolatti G (1995) Motor facilitation during action observation: a magnetic stimulation study. J Neurophysiol 73: 2608–2611.

Fogassi L, Gallese V, Fadiga L, Rizzolatti G (1998) Neurons responding to the sight of goal directed hand/arm actions in the parietal area PF (7b) of the macaque monkey. Soc Neurosci Abs 24:257.5.

Frith U, Frith CD (2003) Development and neurophysiology of mentalizing. Philos Trans R Soc Lond B Biol Sci 358: 459.

Frontera JG (1956) Some results obtained by electrical stimulation of the cortex of the island of Reil in the brain of the monkey (Macaca mulatta). J Comp Neurol 105: 365–394.

Farah, M.J. (1989), 'The neural basis of mental imagery', Trends in Neurosciences, 10.

Finlay BL, Darlington RB (1995) Linked regularities in the development and evolution of mammalian brains. Science 268.

Freud, S. "The Interpretation of Dreams", 1900

Freud, S. "Selected papers on hysteria and other psychoneuroses" Journal of Nervous and Mental Disease 1909.

Freud, S. "The Origin and Development of Psychoanalysis", 1910

Freud, S. "Psychopathology of everyday life", 1914

Freud, S. "Beyond the Pleasure Principle", 1920

Frith, C.D. & Dolan, R.J. (1997), 'Abnormal beliefs: Delusions and memory', Paper presented at the May, 1997, Harvard Conference on Memory and Belief.

Gay, Volney, ed. Neuroscience and Religion. Plymouth, UK: Lexington Books, 2009.

Gazzaniga, M. S. (1985). The social brain. New York: Basic Books.

Gazzaniga, M.S. (1993), 'Brain mechanisms and conscious experience', Ciba Foundation Symposium, 174.

Geschwind N. "Behavioural changes in temporal lobe epilepsy". Psychol Med. 1979.

Gellhorn, E., Kiely, W.F. "Mystical states of consciousness: neurophysiological and clinical aspects." J Nerv Ment Dis. 1972;154:399-405.

Gilbert SL, Dobyns WB, Lahn BT (2005) Genetic links between brain development and brain evolution. Nat Rev Genet 6.

Gray JA. The Psychology of Fear and Stress. 2nd ed. New York, NY: Cambridge University Press; 1988.

Gray JA. The Neuropsychology of Anxiety: An Enquiry into the Functions of the Septo Hippocampal System. 2nd ed. New York, NY: Oxford University Press; 2003.

Gloor, P. (1992), 'Amygdala and temporal lobe epilepsy', in The Amygdala: Neurobiological Aspects of Emotion, Memory and Mental Dysfunction, ed J.P. Aggleton (New York: Wiley-Liss).

Greenspan, S. I. and S. G. Shanker (2004). The first idea: How symbols, language, and intelligence evolved from our early primate ancestors to modern humans. Cambridge, MA: Da Capo Press.

Grady, D. (1993), 'The vision thing: Mainly in the brain', Discover, June.

Graham DT. Prediction of fainting in blood donors. Circulation. 1961;23:901-906.

Grubb BP, Olshansky B. Syncope: Mechanisms and Management. 1st ed. New York, NY: Futura Publishing Company; 1998.

Gallagher HL, Frith CD (2003) Functional imaging of 'theory of mind'. Trends Cogn Sci 7: 77.

Gallese V, Fogassi L, Fadiga L, Rizzolatti G (2002) Action representation and the inferior parietal lobule. In: Prinz W, Hommel B (eds) Attention & Performance XIX. Common mechanisms in perception and action. Oxford University Press, Oxford.

Gallese V, Keysers C, Rizzolatti G (2004) A unifying view of the basis of social cognition. Trends Cogn Sci 8: 396–403.

Gangitano M, Mottaghy FM, Pascual-Leone A (2001) Phase specific modulation of cortical motor output during movement observation. NeuroReport 12: 1489–1492.

Gangitano M, Mottaghy FM, Pascual-Leone A (2004) Modulation of premotor mirror neuron activity during observation of unpredictable grasping movements. Eur J Neurosci 20: 2193–2202.

Goldman AI, Sripada CS (2004) Simulationist models of face-based emotion recognition. Cognition 94: 193–213.

Grafton ST, Arbib MA, Fadiga L, Rizzolatti G (1996) Localization of grasp representations in humans by PET: 2. Observation compared with imagination. Exp Brain Res 112: 103–111.

Grèzes J, Costes N, Decety J (1998) Top-down effect of strategy on the perception of human biological motion: a PET investigation. Cogn Neuropsychol 15: 553–582.

Grèzes J, Armony JL, Rowe J, Passingham RE (2003) Activations related to "mirror" and "canonical" neurones in the human brain: an fMRI study. Neuroimage 18: 928–937.

Gross CG, Rocha-Miranda CE, Bender DB (1972) Visual properties of neurons in the inferotemporal cortex of the macaque. J Neurophysiol 35: 96–111.

Hari R, Forss N, Avikainen S, Kirveskari S, Salenius S, Rizzolatti G (1998) Activation of human primary motor cortex during action observation: a neuromagnetic study. Proc. Natl Acad Sci USA 95: 15061–15065.

Hall, Daniel, Keith Meador, and Harold Koenig. "Measuring Religiousness in Health Research: Review and Critique." Journal of Religion and Health 47, no. 2 (2008)

Harris, Sam, Jonas Kaplan, Ashley Curiel, Susan Bookheimer, Marco Iacoboni, and Mark Cohen. "The Neural Correlates of Religious and Nonreligious Belief." PLoS One 4, no. 10 (October 1, 2009)

Halgren, E. (1992), 'Emotional neurophysiology of the amygdala within the context of human cognition', in The Amygdala: Neurobiological Aspects of Emotion, Memory and Mental Dysfunction, ed J.P. Aggleton (New York: Wiley-Liss).

Halligan PW, Fink GR, Marshal JC, Vallar G. 2003. Spatial cognition: evidence from visual neglect. Trends Cogn Sci.

Handbook of Emotions, Edited by Michael Lewis, Jeannette M. Haviland-Jones, and Lisa Feldman Barrett, The Guilford Press; 3rd edition (2010).

Haggard, P., Clark, S. and Kalogeras,]. (2002) Voluntary action and conscious awareness, Nature Neuroscience 5, 382-5. Haggard, P., Newman, C. and Magno, E. (1999) On the perceived time of voluntary actions. British Journal of Psychology 90, 291-303.

Hameroff, S.R. and Penrose, R. (1996) Conscious events as orchestrated space-time selections. Journal of Consciousness Studies 3(1), 36-53; also reprinted in J. Shear (ed.) (1997) Explaining Consciousness-The Hard Problem. Cambridge, MA, MIT Press, 177-95.

Hardcastle, V.G. (2000) How to understand theN in NCC. InT. Metzinger (ed.) Neural Correlates of Consciousness. Cambridge, MA, MIT Press, 259-64.

Harding, D.E. (1961) On Having no Head: Zen and the Re-Discovery of the Obvious. London, Buddhist Society.

Hardy, A. (1979) The Spiritual Nature of Man: A Study of Contemporary Religious Experience. Oxford, Clarendon Press.

Hamad, S. (1990) The symbol grounding problem. Physica D 42, 335-46.

Hamad, S. (2001) No easy way out. The Sciences 41(2), 36-42.

Harre, R. and Gillett, G. (1994) The Discursive Mind. Thousand Oaks, CA, Sage.

Haugeland, J. (ed.) (1997) Mind Design II: Philosophy, Psychology, Artificial Intelligence. Cambridge, MA, MIT Press.

Hauser, M.D. (2000) Wild Minds: What Animals Really Think. New York, Henry Holt and Co.; London, Penguin.

Hearne, K. (1990) The Dream Machine. Northants, Aquarian.

Hebb, D.O. (1949) The Organization of Behavior. New York, Wiley.

Helmholtz, H.L.F. von (1856-67) Treatise on Physiological Optics.

Heyes, C.M. (1998) Theory of mind in nonhuman primates. Behavioral and Brain Sciences 21, 101-48; with commentaries.

Heyes, C.M. and Galef, B.G. (eds) (1996) Social Learning in Animals: The Roots of Culture. San Diego, CA, Academic Press.

Hitler Adolf, (1925) Mein Kampf, Franz Eher Nachfolger

Hilgard, E.R. (1986) Divided Consciousness: Multiple Controls in Human Thought and Action. New York, Wiley.

Hodgson, R. (1891) A case of double consciousness. Proceedings of the

Society for Psychical Research 7, 221-58.

Hofstadter, D.R. (1979) Code!, Escher, Bach: An Eternal Golden Braid. London, Penguin.

Hofstadter, D.R. and Dennett, D.C. (eds) (1981) The Mind's I: Fantasies and Reflections on Self and Soul. London, Penguin.

Holland, J. (ed.) (2001) Ecstasy: The Complete Guide: A Comprehensive Look at the Risks and Benefits of MDMA. Rochester, VT, Park Street Press.

Holmes, D.S. (1987) The influence of meditation versus rest on physiological arousal. In M. West (ed.) The Psychology of Meditation. Oxford, Clarendon Press, 81-103.

Holt, J. (1999) Blindsight in debates about qualia. Journal of Consciousness Studies 6(5), 54-71.

Horgan, J. (1994), 'Can science explain consciousness?', Scientific American, 271.

Holloway RL (1996) Evolution of the human brain. In: Lock A, Peters CR (eds) Handbook of human symbolic evolution. Oxford University Press, Oxford

Iacoboni M, Woods RP, Brass M, Bekkering H, Mazziotta JC, Rizzolatti G (1999) Cortical mechanisms of human imitation. Science 286: 2526–2528.

Iacoboni M, Koski LM, Brass M, Bekkering H, Woods RP, Dubeau MC, Mazziotta JC, Rizzolatti G (2001) Reafferent copies of imitated actions in the right superior temporal cortex. Proc Natl Acad Sci USA 98: 13995–13999.

Jeannerod M (1988) The neural and behavioural organization of goal-directed movements. Clarendon Press, Oxford.

Johnson-Frey SH, Maloof FR, Newman-Norlund R, Farrer C, Inati S, Grafton ST (2003) Actions or hand-objects interactions? Human inferior frontal cortex and action observation. Neuron 39: 1053–1058.

Jackson, F. (1982) Epiphenomenal qualia. Philosophical Quarterly 32, 127-36.

James, W. (1890) The Principles of Psychology (2 volumes). London, Macmillan.

James, W. (1902) The Varieties of Religious Experience: A Study in Human Nature. New York and London, Longmans, Green and Co.

Jansen, K. (2001) Ketamine: Dreams and Realities. Sarasota, FL, Multidisciplinary Association for Psychedelic Studies.

Jay, M. (ed.) (1999) Artificial Paradises: A Drugs Reader. London, Penguin.

Jaynes, J. (1976) The Origin of Consciousness in the Breakdown of the Bicameral Mind. New York, Houghton Mifflin.

Johnson, M.K. and Raye, C.L. (1981) Reality monitoring. Psychological Review 88, 67-85.

Julien, R.M. (2001) A Primer of Drug Action: A Concise, Nontechnical Guide to the Actions, Uses, and Side Effects of Psychoactive Drugs (revised edn). New York, Henry Holt.

Kaada BR, Pribram KH, Epstein JA (1949) Respiratory and vascular responses in monkeys from temporal pole, insula, orbital surface and cingulate gyrus: a preliminary report. J Neurophysiol 12: 347–356.

Kohler E, Keysers C, Umiltà MA, Fogassi L, Gallese V, Rizzolatti G (2002). Hearing sounds, understanding actions: action Rrepresentation in mirror neurons. Science 297: 846–848.

Koski L, Wohlschlager A, Bekkering H, Woods RP, Dubeau MC (2002) Modulation of motor and premotor activity during imitation of target-directed actions. Cereb Cortex 12: 847–855.

Koski L, Iacoboni M, Dubeau MC, Woods RP, Mazziotta JC (2003) Modulation of cortical activity during different imitative behaviors. J Neurophysiol 89: 460–471.

Krolak-Salmon P, Henaff MA, Isnard J, Tallon-Baudry C, Guenot M, Vighetto A, Bertrand O, Mauguiere F (2003) An attention modulated response to disgust in human ventral anterior insula. Ann Neurol 53: 446–453.

Kandel, E. R. In Search of Memory: The Emergence of a New Science of Mind, W. W. Norton & Company (2007).

Kandel E. R. Schwartz JH, Jessel TM. Principles of neural sciences. New York; McGraw Hill, 2000.

Kanizsa, G. (1979), Organization In Vision (New York: Praeger).

Kaloupek DG, Scott JR, Khatami V. Assessment of coping strategies associated with syncope in blood donors. J Psychosom Res. 1985;29:207-214.

Kanwisher, N. (2001) Neural events and perceptual awareness. Cognition 79, 89-113; also reprinted inS. Dehaene (ed.) The Cognitive Neuroscience of Consciousness. Cambridge, MA, MIT Press, 89-113.

Kapleau, Roshi P. (1980) The Three Pillars of Zen: Teaching, Practice, and Enlightenment (revised edn). New York, Doubleday.

Karn, K. and Hayhoe, M. (2000) Memory representations guide

targeting eye movements in a natural task. Visual Cognition 7, 673-703.

Kasamatsu, A. and Hirai, T. (1966) An electroencephalographic study on the Zen meditation (zazen). Folia Psychiatrica et Neurologica Japonica 20, 315-36.

Kaiserman-Abramof, I. R., Graybiel, A. M., & Nauta, W. J. (1980). The thalamic projection to cortical area 17 in a congenitally anophthalmic mouse strain. Neuroscience, 5, 41–52.

Kanold, P. O., Kara, P., Reid, R. C., & Shatz, C. J. (2003). Role of subplate neurons in functional maturation of visual cortical columns. Science, 301, 521–525.

Kennedy, H., & Dehay, C. (1988). Functional implications of the anatomical organization of the callosal projections of visual areas V1 and V2 in the macaque monkey. Behav. Brain Res., 29, 225–236.

Kennedy, H., & Dehay, C. (1993). Cortical specifi cation of mice and men. Cereb. Cortex, 3, 171–186.

Koketsu, D., Mikami, A., Miyamoto, Y., & Hisatsune, T. (2003). Nonrenewal of neurons in the cerebral neocortex of adult macaque monkeys. J. Neurosci., 23, 937–942.

Komuro, H., & Rakic, P. (1992). Selective role of N-type calcium channels in neuronal migration. Science, 257, 806–809.

Komuro, H., & Rakic, P. (1993). Modulation of neuronal migration by NMDA receptors. Science, 260, 95–97.

Komuro, H., & Rakic, P. (1996). Intracellular Ca2+ fl uctuations modulate the rate of neuronal migration. Neuron, 17, 275–285.

Kornack, D. R., & Rakic, P. (1995). Radial and horizontal deployment of clonally related cells in the primate neocortex: Relation- ship to distinct mitotic lineages. Neuron, 15, 311–321.

Kornack, D. R., & Rakic, P. (1999). Continuation of neurogenesis in the hippocampus of the adult macaque monkey. Proc. Natl. Acad. Sci. USA, 96, 5768–5773.

Kornack, D. R., & Rakic, P. (2001a). Cell proliferation without neurogenesis in adult primate neocortex. Science, 294, 2127–2130.

Kornack, D. R., & Rakic, P. (2001b). The generation, migration, and differentiation of olfactory neurons in the adult primate brain. Proc. Natl. Acad. Sci. USA, 98, 4752–4757.

Kostovic, I., & Molliver, D. E. (1974). A new interpretation of the laminar development of cerebral cortex: Synaptogenesis in different layers of neopalium in the human fetus. Anat. Rec., 178, 395.

Kostovic, I., & Rakic, P. (1980). Cytology and time of origin of interstitial neurons in the white matter in infant and adult human and monkey telencephalon. J. Neurocytol., 9, 219–242.

Kostovic, I., & Rakic, P. (1984). Development of prestriate visual projections in the monkey and human fetal cerebrum revealed by transient cholinesterase staining. J. Neurosci., 4, 25–42.

Kennett, J. (1972) Selling Water by the River. London, Allen & Unwin; also published by New York, Vintage.

Kentridge, R.W. and Heywood, C.A. (1999) The status of blindsight. Journal of Consciousness Studies 6(5), 3-11.

Kihlstrom, J.F. (1996) Perception without awareness of what is perceived, learning without awareness of what is learned. In M. Velmans (ed.)

The Science of Consciousness. London, Routledge, 23-46.

Kluver, H. (1926) Mescal visions and eidetic vision. American Journal of Psychology 37, 502-15.

Kollerstrom, N. (1999) The path of Halley's comet, and Newton's late apprehension of the law of gravity. Annals of Science 56, 331-56.

Kosslyn, S.M. (1980) Image and Mind. Cambridge, MA, Harvard University Press.

Kosslyn, S.M. (1988) Aspects of a cognitive neuroscience of mental imagery. Science 240, 1621-6.

Kinsbourne, M. (1995), 'The intralaminar thalamic nucleii', Consciousness and Cognition, 4.

Kjaer, Troels, Camilla Bertelsen, Paola Piccini, David Brooks, Jorgen Alving, and Hans Lou. "Increased Dopamine Tone during Meditation- Induced

Change of Consciousness." Cognitive Brain Research 13, no. 2 (April 2002)

Kölmel HW. 1985. Complex visual hallucinations in the hemianopic field. J Neurol Neurosurg Psychiatry.

Koenig, Harold. "Research on Religion, Spirituality, and Mental Health: A Review." Canadian Journal of Psychiatry 54, no. 5 (May 2009)

Koenig, Harold, ed. Handbook of Religion and Mental Health. San Diego, CA: Academic Press, 1998

Kraepelin E. Psychiatry: A Textbook for Students and Physicians. New York, NY: Science History Publications; 1990.

Lauglin, Charles, John McManus, and Eugene d'Aquili. Brain, Symbol, and Experience. 2nd ed. New York: Columbia University Press, 1992

Lakoff, G. and M. Johnson (1999). Philosophy in the flesh. Basic Books: New York.

LeDoux, J. E. (1996). The emotional brain. New York: Simon & Schuster.

LeDoux, J.E. (1992), 'Emotion and the amygdala', in The Amygdala: Neurobiological Aspects of Emo- tion, Memory and Mental Dysfunction, ed J.P. Aggleton (New York: Wiley-Liss).

Levin, D.T. and Simons, D.J. (1997) Failure to detect changes to attended objects in motion pictures. Psychonomic Bulletin and Review 4, 501-6.

Levine,J. (1983) Materialism and qualia: the explanatory gap. Pacific Philosophical Quarterly 64, 354-61.

Levine,J. (2001) Purple Haze: The Puzzle of Consciousness. New York, Oxford University Press. Levine, S. (1979) A Gradual Awakening. New York, Doubleday.

Levinson, B.W. (1965) States of awareness during general anaesthesia. British Journal of Anaesthesia 37, 544-6.

Lewicki, P., Czyzewska, M. and Hoffman, H. (1987) Unconscious acquisition of complex procedural knowledge. Journal of Experimental Psychology: Learning, Memory and Cognition 13, 523-30.

Lewicki, P., Hill, T. and Bizot, E. (1988) Acquisition of procedural knowledge about a pattern of stimuli that cannot be articulated. Cognitive Psychology 20, 24-37.

Lewicki, P., Hill, T. and Czyzewska, M. (1992) Nonconscious acquisition of information. American Psychologist 47, 796-801.

Manthey S, Schubotz RI, von Cramon DY (2003). Premotor cortex in observing erroneous action: an fMRI study. Brain Res Cogn Brain Res 15: 296–307.

Marx Karl, Engels Friedrich, (1848) The Communist Manifesto

Mesulam MM, Mufson EJ (1982) Insula of the old world monkey. III: Efferent cortical output and comments on function. J Comp Neurol 212: 38–52.

Naskar, Abhijit. "What is Mind?", 2016

Naskar, Abhijit. "In Search of Divinity: Journey to The Kingdom of Conscience", 2016

Naskar, Abhijit. "Love, God & Neurons: Memoir of A Scientist who found himself by getting lost", 2016

Naskar, Abhijit. "Neurons of Jesus: Mind of A Teacher, Spouse & Thinker", 2017

Naskar, Abhijit. "The Education Decree", 2017

Naskar, Abhijit. "Principia Humanitas", 2017

Naskar, Abhijit. "Either Civilized or Phobic: A Treatise on Homosexuality", 2017

Naskar, Abhijit. "We Are All Black: A Treatise on Racism", 2017

Naskar, Abhijit. "Wise Mating: A Treatise on Monogamy", 2017

Naskar, Abhijit. "Illusion of Religion: A Treatise on Religious Fundamentalism", 2017

Naskar, Abhijit. "I Am The Thread: My Mission", 2017

Naskar, Abhijit. "Morality Absolute", 2017

Naskar, Abhijit. "Time to Save Medicine", 2018

Naskar, Abhijit. "Fabric of Humanity", 2018

Naskar, Abhijit. "Build Bridges not Walls: In the name of Americana", 2018

Naskar, Abhijit. "The Constitution of The United Peoples of Earth", 2019

Newberg, Andrew, and Jeremy Iversen. "The Neural Basis of the Complex Mental Task of Meditation:

Neurotransmitter and Neurochemical Considerations." Medical Hypotheses 61, no. 2 (2003).

Newberg, Andrew. "How God Changes Your Brain: An Introduction to Jewish Neurotheology", CCAR Journal: The Reform Jewish Quarterly, Winter 2016.

Newberg, Andrew, and Stephanie Newberg. "A Neuropsychological Perspective on Spiritual Development." In Handbook of Spiritual Development in Childhood and Adolescence, edited by Eugene Roehlkepartain, Pamela King, Linda Wagener, and Peter Benson. London: Sage Publications, Inc., 2005

Newberg, Andrew. "The Neurotheology Link An Intersection Between Spirituality and Health", Alternative and Complimentary Therapies, Vol 21 No 1, February 2015.

Newberg, Andrew, Nancy Wintering, Dharma Khalsa, Hannah Roggenkamp, and Mark Waldman. "Meditation Effects on Cognitive Function and Cerebral Blood Flow in Subjects with Memory Loss: A Preliminary Study." Journal of Alzheimer's Disease 20, no. 2 (2010)

Nash, M. (1995), 'Glimpses of the mind', Time.

Nesse RM. Proximate and evolutionary studies of anxiety, stress and depression: synergy at the interface. Neurosci Biobehav Rev. 1999;23:895-903.

Nishitani N, Hari R (2000) Temporal dynamics of cortical representation for action. Proc Natl Acad Sci USA 97: 913–918.

Nishitani N, Hari R (2002) Viewing lip forms: cortical dynamics. Neuron 36: 1211–1220.

Obama Barack, (2006) The Audacity of Hope: Thoughts on Reclaiming the American Dream, Crown/Three Rivers Press

O'Hara, K. and Scutt, T. (1996) There is no hard problem of consciousness. Journal of Consciousness Studies 3(4), 290-302, reprinted in J. Shear (ed.) (1997) Explaining Consciousness. Cambridge, MA, MIT Press, 69-82.

O'Regan, J.K. (1992) Solving the "real" mysteries of visual perception: the world as an outside memory. Canadian Journal of Psychology 46, 461-88.

O'Regan, J.K. and Noe, A. (2001) A sensorimotor account of vision and visual consciousness. Behavioral and Brain Sciences 24(5), 883-917.

O'Regan, J.K., Rensink, R.A. and Clark,].]. (1999) Change-blindness as a result of "mudsplashes." Nature 398, 34.

Ornstein, R.E. (1977) The Psychology of Consciousness (2nd edn). New York, Harcourt.

Ornstein, R.E. (1986) The Psychology of Consiousness (3rd edn). New York, Pehguin.

Ornstein, R.E. (1992) The Evolution of Consciousness. New York, Touchstone.

Penfield W, Faulk ME (1955) The insula: further observations on its function. Brain 78: 445– 470.

Penrose, R. (1994), Shadows of the Mind (Oxford: Oxford University Press).

Penrose, R. (1989), The Emperor's New Mind: Concerning Computers, Minds and The Laws of Physics (Oxford: Oxford University Press).

Persinger, "'I would kill in God's name' role of sex, weekly church attendance, report of a religious experience and limbic lability" Perceptual and Motor Skills 1997.

Persinger "Experimental simulation of the God experience" Neurotheology 2003.

Persinger, M. A. (1993b). Personality changes following brain injury as a grief response to the loss of sense of self: Phenomenological themes as indices of local lability and neurocognitive restructuring as psycho- therapy. Psychological Reports, 72

Persinger, Corradini, Clement, Keaney, et al "Neurotheology and its convergence with neuroquantology" NeuroQuantology 2010.

Persinger, Koren and St-Pierre "The electromagnetic induction of mystical and altered states within the laboratory" Journal of Consciousness Exploration and Research 2010.

Persinger "Case report: A prototypical spontaneous 'sensed presence' of a sentient being and concomitant electroencephalographic activity in the clinical laboratory" Neurocase 2008.

Persinger and Saroka "Potential production of Hughlings Jackson's "parasitic consciousness" by physiologically-patterned weak transcerebral magnetic fields: QEEG and source localization" Epilepsy & Behavior 28 (2013).

Persinger. "The neuropsychiatry of paranormal experiences". J Neuropsychiatry Clin Neurosci 2001.

Persinger. "Neuropsychological bases of god beliefs", New York: Praeger, 1987

Persinger. "Temporal lobe epileptic signs and correlative behaviors displayed by normal populations", Journal of General Psychology, 1986

Persinger "Experimental Facilitation of the Sensed Presence: Possible Intercalation between the Hemispheres Induced by Complex Magnetic Fields" Journal of Nervous and Mental Disease 2002.

Plato, Republic, 381 BC

Page AC. Blood-injury phobia. Clinical Psychology Review. 1994;14:443-461.

Perry BD, Pollard R. Homeostasis, stress, trauma, and adaptation. A neurodevelopmental view of childhood trauma. Child Adolesc Psychiatr Clin N Am. 1998;7:33.

Paré, D. & Llinás, R. (1995), 'Conscious and preconscious processes as seen from the standpoint of sleep-waking cycle neurophysiology', Neuropsychologia, 33.

P. S. de Laplace. Essai Philosophique sur les Probabilites [1814], in Academy des Sciences, Oeuvres Complotes de

Laplace, Vol. 7, Gauthier-Villars, Paris (1886).

Perrett DI, Harries MH, Bevan R, Thomas S, Benson PJ, Mistlin AJ, Chitty AJ, Hietanen JK, Ortega JE (1989) Frameworks of analysis for the neural representation of animate objects and actions. J Exp Bio 146: 87–113.

Phillips ML, Young AW, Senior C, Brammer M, Andrew C, Calder AJ, Bullmore ET, Perrett DI, Rowland D, Williams SC, Gray JA, David AS (1997) A specific neural substrate for perceiving facial expressions of disgust. Nature 389: 495–498.

Phillips ML, Young AW, Scott SK, Calder AJ, Andrew C, Giampietro V, Williams SC, Bullmore ET, Brammer M, Gray JA (1998) Neural responses to facial and vocal expressions of fear and disgust. Proc R Soc Lond B Biol Sci 265: 1809–1817.

Puce A, Perrett D (2003) Electrophysiological and brain imaging of biological motion. Philosoph Trans Royal Soc Lond, Series B, 358: 435–445.

Ramachandran VS. Behavioral and magnetoencephalographic correlates of plasticity in the adult human brain. Proc Natl Acad Sci USA 1993; 90: 10413–20.

Ramachandran VS. Phantom limbs, neglect syndromes, repressed memories, and Freudian psychology. Int Rev Neurobiol 1994; 37: 291–333.

Ramachandran VS. Plasticity and functional recovery in neurology. Clin Med 2005; 5: 368–73.

Ramachandran VS, Hirstein W. The perception of phantom limbs. The D. O. Hebb lecture. Brain 1998; 121: 1603–30.

Ramachandran VS, McGeoch PD, Williams L, Arcilla G. Rapid relief of thalamic pain syndrome induced by vestibular caloric stimulation. Neurocase 2007; 13: 185–8.

Ramachandran VS, Rogers-Ramachandran D, Cobb S. Touching the phantom limb. Nature 1995; 377: 489–90.

Ramachandran VS, Rogers-Ramachandran D. Phantom limbs and neural plasticity. Arch Neurol 2000; 57: 317–20.

Ramachandran VS, Rogers-Ramachandran D. It's all done with mirrors. Sci Am Mind 2007; 18: 16–9.

Ramachandran VS, Rogers-Ramachandran D. Sensations referred to a patient's phantom arm from another subjects intact arm: perceptual correlates of mirror neurons. Med Hypotheses 2008; 70: 1233–4.

Ramachandran VS, Rogers-Ramachandran D, Stewart M. Perceptual correlates of massive

cortical reorganization. Science 1992;
258: 1159–60.

Rizzolatti G, Craighero L (2004) The
mirror-neuron system. Annu Rev
Neurosci 27: 169–192.

Rizzolatti G, Scandolara C, Matelli M,
Gentilucci M (1981) Afferent
properties of periarcuate neurons in
macaque monkeys. I. Somatosensory
responses. Behav Brain Res 2: 125–146.

Rizzolatti G, Fadiga L, Matelli M,
Bettinardi V, Paulesu E, Perani D,
Fazio F (1996) Localization of grasp
representation in humans by PET: 1.
Observation versus execution. Exp
Brain Res 111: 246–252.

Rizzolatti G, Fogassi L, Gallese V
(2001) Neurophysiological
mechanisms underlying the
understanding and imitation of action.
Nature Rev Neurosci 2:661–670.

Rock I, Victor J. Vision and touch: an
experimentally created conflict

between the two senses. Science 1964; 143: 594–6.

Rose'n B, Lundborg G. Training with a mirror in rehabilitation of the hand. Scand J Plast Reconstr Surg Hand Surg 2005; 39: 104–8.

Royet JP, Plailly J, Delon-Martin C, Kareken DA, Segebarth C (2003) fMRI of emotional responses to odors: influence of hedonic valence and judgment, handedness, and gender. Neuroimage 20: 713–728.

Rozin R Haidt J and McCauley CR (2000) Disgust. In: Lewis M, Haviland-Jones JM (eds) Handbook of Emotion. 2nd Edition. Guilford Press, New York, pp 637–653.

Saxe R, Carey S, Kanwisher N (2004) Understanding other minds: linking developmental psychology and functional neuroimaging. Annu Rev Psychol 55: 87–124.

Schienle A, Stark R, Walter B, Blecker C, Ott U, Kirsch P, Sammer G, Vaitl D (2002) The insula is not specifically involved in disgust processing: an fMRI study. Neuroreport 13: 2023–2026.

Showers MJC, Lauer EW (1961) Somatovisceral motor patterns in the insula. J Comp Neurol 117: 107–115.

Singer T, Seymour B, O'Doherty J, Kaube H, Dolan RJ, Frith CD (2004) Empathy for pain involves the affective but not the sensory components of pain. Science 303: 1157–1162.

Small DM, Gregory MD, Mak YE, Gitelman D, Mesulam MM, Parrish T (2003) Dissociation of neural representation of intensity and affective valuation in human gustation Neuron 39: 701–711.

Smith A (1759) The theory of moral sentiments (ed. 1976). Clarendon Press, Oxford.

Sprengelmeyer R, Rausch M, Eysel UT, Przuntek H (1998) Neural structures associated with recognition of facial expressions of basic emotions Proc R Soc Lond B Biol Sci 265: 1927–1931.

Strafella AP, Paus T (2000) Modulation of cortical excitability during action observation: a transcranial magnetic stimulation study. NeuroReport 11: 2289–2292.

Tanaka K (1996) Inferotemporal cortex and object vision. Ann Rev Neurosci. 19: 109–140.

Tomasello M, Call J (1997) Primate cognition. Oxford University Press, Oxford.

Tremblay C, Robert M, Pascual-Leone A, Lepore F, Nguyen DK, Carmant L, Bouthillier A, Theoret H (2004) Action observation and execution: intracranial recordings in a human subject. Neurology. 63: 937–938.

Umilta MA, Kohler E, Gallese V, Fogassi L, Fadiga L, Keysers C, Rizzolatti G (2001) "I know what you are doing": a neurophysiological study. Neuron 32: 91–101.

Visalberghi E, Fragaszy D. (2002). Do monkeys ape? Ten years after. In: Dautenhahn K, Nehaniv C (eds) Imitation in animals and artifacts. MIT Press, Boston. Pp. 471–500

Wicker B, Keysers C, Plailly J, Royet JP, Gallese V, Rizzolatti G (2003) Both of us disgusted in my insula: the common neural basis of seeing and feeling disgust. Neuron 40: 655–664.

Yokochi H, Tanaka M, Kumashiro M, Iriki A (2003) Inferior parietal somatosensory neurons coding face-hand coordination in Japanese macaques. Somatosens Mot Res 20 : 115–125.

Zald DH, Pardo JV (2000) Functional neuroimaging of the olfactory system in humans. Int J Psychophysiol 36: 165–181.

Zald DH, Donndelinger MJ, Pardo JV (1998) Elucidating dynamic brain interactions with across-subjects correlational analyses of positron emission tomographic data: the functional connectivity of the amygdala and orbitofrontal cortex during olfactory tasks. J Cereb Blood Flow Metab 18: 896–905.

ABHIJIT NASKAR